FACTOURISM

FACTOURISM

An Illustrated Journey of Funny, Horrible,
and Unbelievable Facts about...Everything

ferdio

Adams Media

New York London Toronto Sydney New Delhi

Aadamsmedia

An Imprint of Simon & Schuster, Inc.
57 Littlefield Street
Avon, Massachusetts 02322

First Adams Media hardcover edition May 2021

ADAMS MEDIA and colophon are trademarks of Simon & Schuster.

For information about special discounts for bulk purchases, please contact Simon & Schuster Special Sales at 1-866-506-1949 or business@simonandschuster.com.

The Simon & Schuster Speakers Bureau can bring authors to your live event. For more information or to book an event contact the Simon & Schuster Speakers Bureau at 1-866-248-3049 or visit our website at www.simonspeakers.com.

Interior design and illustrations by Ferdio

Manufactured in China

10 9 8 7 6 5 4 3 2 1

Library of Congress Cataloging-in-Publication Data has been applied for.

ISBN 978-1-5072-1431-2
ISBN 978-1-5072-1432-9 (ebook)

INTRODUCTION

Did you know that ketchup was once sold as medicine for digestive disorders? That the human body contains gold? That there are no stop signs in Paris?

The world is a fascinating place. Here at *Factourism* we combine curious facts with our love of illustration to create visual tidbits that will intrigue you, make you laugh, or perhaps horrify you. This book covers all kinds of interesting topics, like nature, pop culture, science, climate, history, and technology. You will discover things you didn't know about pizzas, selfies, saliva, IKEA, Nutella, and even ferrets. Each fun and intriguing page features a piece of trivia that will leave you brimming with knowledge.

Get ready to take a tour around the world—one strange fact at a time!

Factourism is a project by Ferdio, an information design agency based in Copenhagen, Denmark. We turn data and information into captivating visuals. Discover our work at Ferdio.com.

Selfies kill more people than sharks

Sharks are not great at killing humans. In 2015, for instance, there were only 8 deaths caused by the toothed fish. That same year, 12 people died from the seemingly harmless pastime of taking a selfie. Four of these deaths occurred when people fell while taking the picture.

Source: *Newsweek*

Six pieces of 2 × 4 LEGO bricks can be combined in **915,103,765** ways

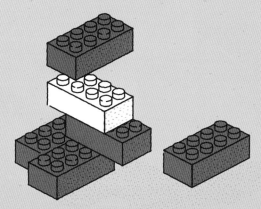

Danish mathematician Søren Eilers wondered how many different structures could be built from 6 classic rectangular bricks. He wrote a computer program calculating all the possibilities and finally got the definitive answer after half a week of computing.

Source: *Mental Floss*

The world's largest pizza was about **3 times** as big as a basketball court

The Nazionale Italiana Pizzaioli has held the record for the largest pizza since 2012, with a surface of 13,580 ft²—and it's gluten-free. For reference, a professional basketball court measures 4,520 ft². The same organization also brewed the world's biggest cappuccino—an 80,000-fluid-ounce coffee cup.

Source: *Guinness World Records*

Babies have **95** more bones than adults

Adult humans usually have 206 bones, but babies have about 300. Many of these, such as the cranium (better known as the skull), begin as several separate parts before merging into 1 when the child grows up. Many baby "bones" are also not exactly bones at this point: They are cartilage and only turn into true bones after some time.

Source: *HowStuffWorks*

A person eats at least **50,000** microplastic particles a year

Researchers have found microscopic plastic particles almost everywhere: in the air, soil, water, food, and even in beverages. To make matters worse, people breathe in about the same amount of microplastics they eat during a year!

Source: *The Guardian*

Men whose age ends in **9** are most prone to cheat

A study analyzed the ages of 8 million users on a website for men seeking extramarital affairs. Almost a million had an age ending with 9, overrepresented by 18 percent compared to other ages. The study also observed other behavioral changes in those with an age ending in 9: more participation in marathons and a higher rate of suicide.

Source: National Academy of Sciences

There are so many varieties of apples that it would take more than **20 years** to taste them all if you ate 1 every day

June 28

June 29

June 30

July 1

July 2

July 3

July 4

More than 7,000 varieties of apples exist today. Some varieties are good for eating, while others are better for cider, jelly, or decoration. Some of the identified varieties are quite old and aren't grown in large quantities anymore.
Source: *Weldon Owen*

Ancient Egyptians played bowling
5,000 years ago

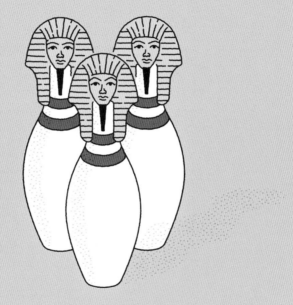

An ancient "bowling hall" with lanes 13 feet long was excavated by archaeologists. It was not exactly bowling as we know it today: One player would throw a stone ball, and another player would attempt to deviate its trajectory with another ball. Bowling-type games remained popular during history, and pins would finally be invented around A.D. 300.

Source: *Ancient Pages*

A doughnut-shaped planet is technically possible

Even if it is extremely unlikely to exist, a planet shaped like a torus—the technical name for the doughnut shape—is not physically impossible. Researchers have made simulations and calculated the gravitational forces implicated, and everything checks out. The weather would be very peculiar, and there could even be moons orbiting through the hole.

Source: *Gizmodo*

A teaspoon of honey is the lifework of **12** bees

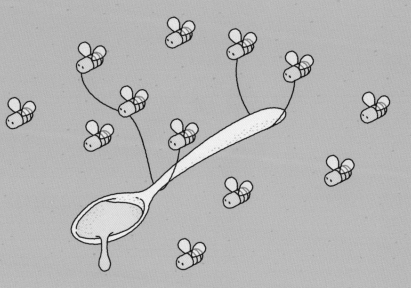

Bees make honey from nectar, the sweet juice of flowery plants. One single worker bee makes on average the equivalent of $1/12$ teaspoon of honey in the bee's entire lifetime. That amount also requires thousands of flowers and many miles of flying between the fields and the hive.

Source: National Honey Board

The Nintendo company existed at the same time as the Ottoman Empire

The Ottoman Empire ruled over Southeast Europe and Western Asia until 1922, when it was dissolved in the aftermath of World War I. In 1889, in Kyoto, Japan, Fusajirō Yamauchi started a new company focused on handmaking playing cards. His business eventually grew to become the video game giant Nintendo.

Source: *Business Insider*

UPS saves **10 million** gallons of gas every year by avoiding left turns

Turning left puts drivers against the flow of vehicles coming the other way, which forces them to wait 30–45 seconds each time, with the engine running. A special routing system, which calculates routes favoring right turns, saves UPS millions of gallons of fuel every year.
Source: CNN

If a car could drive straight up, it would take an hour to get to space

SPACE 62 MI

Where does the atmosphere end and outer space start? Simple answer: at an altitude of 100 kilometers, or 62 miles. This boundary is named the Kármán line, after the physicist who calculated the altitude at which the atmosphere is too thin to support aircrafts. So a car driving 62 mph would get to space in an hour.

Source: *BBC Science Focus*

In 2014, Tinder got its first match in Antarctica

Two scientists in Antarctica—one staying in a tent at a field camp and the other housed at a research station—had the same idea: Check their Tinder account for prospects. Lo and behold, the app was able to match them with someone on the continent. They only managed to meet once, just before one of them was leaving the continent.

Source: *The Cut*

Women's voices have deepened
23 hertz over 5 decades

(due to gender equality)

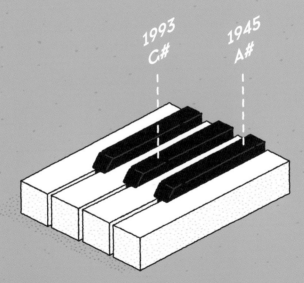

1993
C#

1945
A#

Thanks to the evolution of gender roles during the past century, women are now speaking in a deeper pitch. Researchers noticed this frequency drop when comparing recordings of women from the 1940s with recordings from women in the 1990s. Scientists think the difference could be due to women holding more authoritative roles in society.

Source: *BBC Worklife*

Kids perform better at boring tasks when dressed as Batman

In an experiment, kids aged 4 and 6 were asked to perform a repetitive task with the option to take breaks playing video games—they didn't persevere for very long at the assignment. But across ages, children did spend more time on the task if they were told to impersonate a character such as Batman.

Source: Society for Research in Child Development

About **4 million** trees are cut down every year in China to make disposable chopsticks

China's national forestry office reports that 3.8 million trees are needed to make the 57 billion disposable pairs of chopsticks the country produces every year. About 45 percent are made of cottonwood, birch, and spruce, and the rest are made from bamboo.

Source: *The New York Times*

The Harvard Library has a book bound in human skin

Anthropodermic bibliopegy is the scientific name for binding books with human skin rather than with leather from an animal. It was a morbid practice that was occasionally done in the 19th century and earlier. The Houghton Library at Harvard University contains one such example, the title *Des Destinées de l'Âme* (*Destinies of the Soul*).

Source: *BBC News*

Most people can hear the difference between hot and cold water when poured, just by the sound it makes

When people were asked to listen to 2 sound clips—of cold water and hot water being poured into identical containers—the vast majority of respondents were able to tell them apart just by listening. About 80 percent of people recognized the cold water sound, and 90 percent could tell the hot water sound. Because the hot water is bubblier, it produces a different frequency.

Source: NPR

The average person produces **5,300** gallons of saliva in a lifetime

The flow rate of saliva in your mouth is about 1 ounce an hour: It is mostly swallowed and reabsorbed, but some new saliva is also produced. That amounts to about a small bottle a day, and a couple of small swimming pools in a life.
Source: *BBC Science Focus*

Pablo Escobar cheated at Monopoly with his kids, hiding extra money ahead of time where he planned to sit

In a documentary, Juan Pablo Escobar recalled his father's unbeatable strategy at Monopoly: planting some of the board game's paper money between the cushions of the family couch or under the living room carpet a few hours before the game (or having an associate do it for him).

Source: *Business Insider*

The most common time to wake up at night is **3:44 a.m.**

A study on the sleeping habits of 3,000 adults figured out that, along with the fact that many people have sleep troubles, 3:44 in the middle of the night was the most common time to wake up.

Source: *Mirror*

Coconut water has been used as an intravenous drip instead of saline in critical emergencies

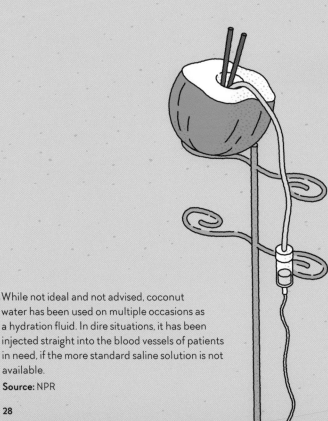

While not ideal and not advised, coconut water has been used on multiple occasions as a hydration fluid. In dire situations, it has been injected straight into the blood vessels of patients in need, if the more standard saline solution is not available.

Source: NPR

Rabbits can smell their dead relatives in the feces of predators

Rabbits can recognize the smell of their predators' feces—and researchers recently discovered that rabbits are also able to distinguish which of those predators have specifically been eating other rabbits. If rabbits find places with lots of rabbit-laced feces, they avoid the area.

Source: *Newsweek*

If you lose your thumb, surgeons can replace it with your big toe

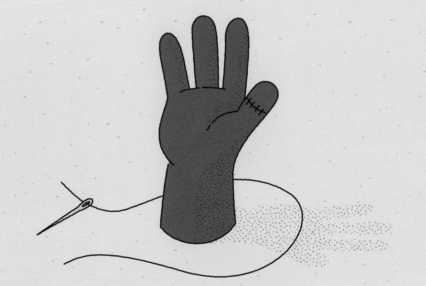

It's an unusual procedure, but it has been done, at least once, in the Netherlands. After a work accident in which he lost his thumb, the patient wanted to continue riding his motorbike. The medical team took off his toe and successfully reconnected vessels, nerves, and tendons to the spot where the thumb previously stood.

Source: News.com.au

Leonardo da Vinci could write with one hand and draw with the other hand

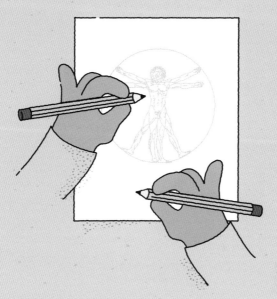

Prolific in sketching and note-taking, Leonardo da Vinci was ambidextrous. He was able to draw and write (in his infamous backward script) with both his left and right hands.

Source: *Discover*

The first computer mouse
was made of wood

Although earlier pointing interfaces did exist, the first to be called a mouse was invented by engineer Douglas Engelbart. Work on the device started in 1963, and the contraption was ready to be demonstrated by 1968. The mouse had wheels (instead of the trackball that was used later) and was, indeed, made of wood.

Source: Mashable

Coca-Cola is used as a pesticide by some farmers in India

Farmers in the Indian state of Chhattisgarh have been using Pepsi or Coca-Cola to protect their rice crops instead of standard pesticides, since the soft drinks are less expensive and get the job done. The sugar attracts ants that feed on other insects and increases the plants' immunity.

Source: *BBC News*

The man who invented pop-up ads has officially apologized to the world

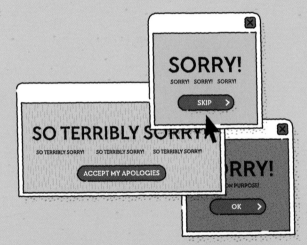

In the 1990s, Ethan Zuckerman was working for a website that displayed ads. But advertisers were not always happy with the pages their banners ended up on. He came up with a solution: opening ads in separate windows. The invention eventually took over the web, bothering users to no end, and Zuckerman publicly apologized.

Source: *Forbes*

Slugs like beer

No, they don't enjoy the taste—slugs are simply attracted to the chemicals emitted from fermentation. Since beer is a very accessible fermented material, it is often used as bait to trap slugs that ruin gardens.

Source: Colorado State University

Nearly all phones in Japan are waterproof, because Japanese women like to use them in the shower

As many as 90–95 percent of mobile phones sold in Japan are waterproof. Why? A manufacturer's executive once said that Japanese women like to keep using them while showering. Because of that, the manufacturers create models that are able to withstand water.

Source: *Daily News* (New York)

Only **5** modern countries were never colonized by Europe

(Japan, North Korea, South Korea, Thailand, and Liberia)

Looking at the history of all contemporary countries, every single one of them minus 5 suffered at one point from colonization, control, influence, or occupation by a European country in one way or another. Japan, North Korea, South Korea, Thailand, and Liberia are the only ones that escaped European colonialism.

Source: *Vox*

The greatest officially recorded number of children born to one mother is **69**

Mrs. Vassilyeva, possibly named Valentina, was a Russian woman who lived in the 18th century. According to *Guinness World Records*, she gave birth to 69 kids, all from the same dad, a man named Feodor. (He later remarried and fathered, he claimed, 18 additional children.) Mrs. Vassilyeva holds the world record for "most prolific mother."

Source: *Guinness World Records*

Thanks to modern TV screens, dogs are able to watch TV as well as humans

Human eyes can register an image flickering at around 55 hertz, while dogs, which are better at detecting quick movements, can see flickering around 75 hertz. Older TV sets showed around 60 images a second, which worked for humans but was too slow for dogs, so the images appeared to flicker rather than being seamless. New TV screens have higher frequencies, so dogs can finally appreciate what happens on TV.

Source: *BBC News*

In Singapore, connecting to someone else's Wi-Fi is illegal and can be punished with up to **3** years of imprisonment

PRISON
WI-FI

● ● ● ● ● ● ●

CONNECT

Singapore is very serious about protecting people's Wi-Fi networks. Using a network without the knowledge of its owner can result in a fine up to 10,000 Singapore dollars (about $7,000), up to 3 years in prison, or both. The first person to be sentenced was a 17-year-old boy who connected to his neighbor's Internet.

Source: *Straits Times*

Ketchup was sold as medicine in the 1830s

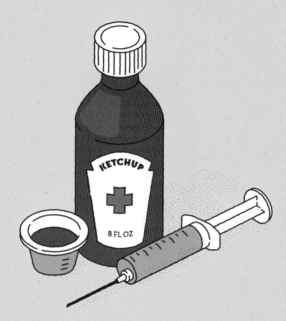

Ketchup dates back to A.D. 544, when it was made in Asia using fish innards. Later, the recipe evolved into an anchovy-based sauce and was introduced to British traders by Chinese sailors. In Britain, the sauce was re-created using beer, walnuts, or mushrooms. Tomato ketchup was finally concocted by an American doctor, who considered it a good treatment for digestive problems.

Source: *Fast Company*

We sigh every **5 minutes** on average; if we didn't, our lungs would collapse

Humans sigh 12 times per hour. It's not always related to being tired or exasperated: Scientists have identified this as a life-sustaining reflex, made to prevent the alveoli in our lungs from collapsing.

Source: *Live Science*

About **28 percent** of delivery drivers have taken food from a customer's order

In a survey, 28 percent of drivers working in food delivery have admitted to tasting a bit of the meal or stealing a French fry or two from the order they were delivering. Luckily for them, only 21 percent of customers ever suspect that it happens.

Source: US Foods

Snails have thousands of teeth

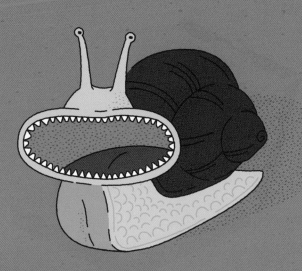

Snails and slugs eat many different things, from plants to insects. That's a lot to chew—or, rather, to rasp. Indeed, instead of a jaw, these gastropods have a flexible band made of thousands of microscopic teeth. Called the radula, it acts as a file and grates down the food.

Source: Natural History Museum

Apple had its own clothing line in 1986

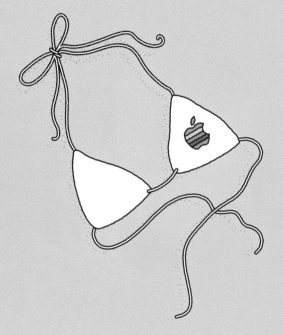

In 1986, the year Steve Jobs left the company, Apple released a fashion line, which included T-shirts, sweatshirts, belts, caps, and jackets—and even windsurfing equipment! All very colorful, the pieces featured either the classic rainbow Apple logo or experimental takes on the name Apple.

Source: *Fast Company*

McDonald's has a ski-through restaurant in Sweden

In the Swedish mountains about 200 miles north of Stockholm, the fast-food company adapted their original drive-through concept to local conditions. They opened a "McSki" service, where skiers can order and pick up their meal without even unfixing their skis or leaving the snow.

Source: *Mental Floss*

You are **14 percent** more likely to die on your birthday than on any other day of the year

Scientists went through a list of 2.5 million deaths between 1969 and 2008 to arrive at this conclusion. They have 2 theories: Either people are participating in activities on their birthday that are more likely to kill them, or absentminded clerks are mistyping the date of birth in the "date of death" field.

Source: *BBC News*

Romans used tickling as torture, with goats licking feet dipped in salt water

Tickling used abusively and without consent quickly becomes torture, and it has been employed throughout human history, from the Romans to the Nazis. The Roman variant using goats was known to be especially painful.

Source: *British Medical Journal*

People fart after they're dead

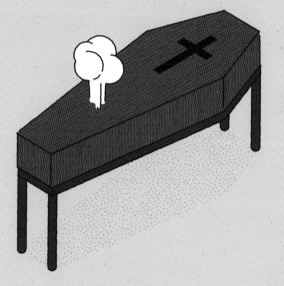

After the immune system shuts down, bacteria present in the digestive tracts invade the blood and tissue of dead bodies. During decomposition, gas is created in the gut, which gets released as farts and burps, especially when the body is being moved.

Source: *Men's Health*

All of the Nutella sold in a year could be spread over more than **1,000** soccer fields

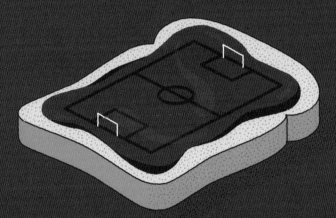

Since it was first created in the 1940s in Italy as "Pasta Gianduja," Nutella has become the most successful hazelnut cocoa spread. Ferrero, the manufacturer, calculated that they sell a jar of Nutella every 2.5 seconds, enough to cover 1,000 soccer fields on a yearly basis if it was spread like on toast.

Source: *Food Beast*

There is a town in Wales called...

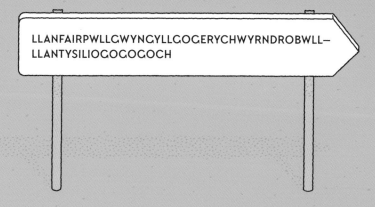

LLANFAIRPWLLGWYNGYLLGOGERYCHWYRNDROBWLL—
LLANTYSILIOGOGOGOCH

The island of Anglesey is home to a town that proudly owns the longest place name in Europe, and the second worldwide. It's a 19-syllable Welsh name given in the 1860s and can be translated in English as "St Mary's Church in the hollow of the white hazel near the rapid whirlpool of the red cave."

Source: *Business Insider*

The average American spends
about **90 percent** of their time indoors

The statistic is part of a study by the US Environmental Protection Agency, in an endeavor not to get more people outside, but to get better air quality inside. The number is not that different in several other places in the world.

Source: US Environmental Protection Agency

A spa house in Japan is offering ramen noodle baths

The Yunessun Spa House in Hakone, Japan, has bathtubs full of soup, pork broth, and noodles. Bathing in the mixture is meant to boost collagen production and increase metabolism.

Source: *Travel + Leisure*

Judges are more likely to grant parole after lunch

Just grant him!

Researchers analyzed the decisions of 8 judges as they made more than a thousand rulings. They found that prisoners being sentenced in the beginning of the day or just after the lunch break were 2–6 times more likely to get a release than the prisoners at other times of the day.

Source: *The Guardian*

There are animals with red, blue, green, yellow, and purple blood

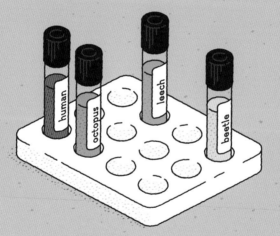

Blood can have different colors depending on its components. Most vertebrates have red blood due to iron. Animals with copper in their blood have blue blood (octopuses, squids, spiders). Vanabin makes blood yellow (beetles, sea cucumbers), chlorocruorin makes green blood (worms, leeches), and hemerythrin leads to purple blood (several types of worms).

Source: *Business Insider*

Self-driving cars learn how to drive better by playing *Grand Theft Auto*

The more self-driving cars self-drive, the better they get at it. But even with a lot of training in the real world, the collected experience isn't enough—so in addition, engineers use simulators...and video games. *Grand Theft Auto*, a video game known for its large-scale city replicas, is the perfect sandbox for a car to learn to navigate.

Source: Bloomberg

There are only **14** possible calendar configurations

(for instance, in 2022, you can reuse a calendar from 2011 and use it again in 2033)

There are 7 configurations for each day that can start the year, times 2 for leap and non-leap years—it's that simple. So search your attic and explore your local thrift shops, and see if you can excavate a calendar to recycle!

Source: *When Can I Reuse This Calendar?*

In the age of the dinosaurs, a day lasted no more than **23 hours**

Earth's rotation has been slowing down, because the gravitational forces exerted by the moon act like a brake. As a consequence, days are getting about 2 milliseconds longer each century. During the Mesozoic era, when dinosaurs lived, a day would have lasted between 21 and 23 hours.

Source: *ABC Science*

The facial expressions of LEGO characters are getting angrier over the years

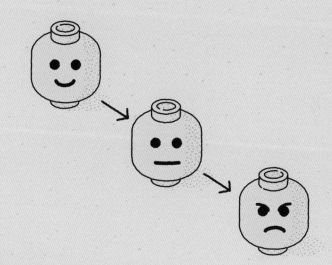

When LEGO mini-figures were introduced in 1978, they were all smiling. However, a 2013 study of 3,655 of these figures revealed that as the years went on, more and more characters featured angry faces. The change might be because more recent LEGO sets include themes that are based on conflict.

Source: *The Guardian*

Drinking too much grape soda will make your poop turn blue

The color of what you eat and drink has an effect on the color of what you excrete, as your body doesn't necessarily digest all the molecules responsible for the coloration of your food. Among the drinks that can make your poop appear bluish are grape juice and grape soda, along with blueberries, currants, and plums.

Source: *Healthline*

Being a bad driver is partially a genetic trait

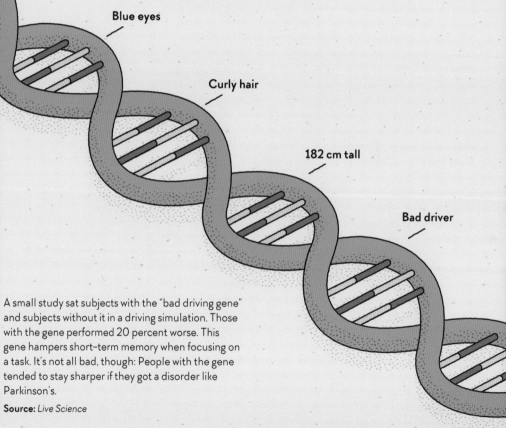

Blue eyes

Curly hair

182 cm tall

Bad driver

A small study sat subjects with the "bad driving gene" and subjects without it in a driving simulation. Those with the gene performed 20 percent worse. This gene hampers short-term memory when focusing on a task. It's not all bad, though: People with the gene tended to stay sharper if they got a disorder like Parkinson's.

Source: *Live Science*

Koalas hug trees to keep cool

Scientists have observed koalas' postures on trees during different weather conditions and have taken thermal photographs showing the distribution of heat in trees and koalas. They found that when it's hot, koalas are more likely to hug trees. Trees have a lower temperature than air, so koalas stay cool by evacuating their body heat to the trunks.

Source: The Royal Society

Eating chocolate could improve your math skills

Chocolate, especially dark varieties, contains flavanols, a form of flavonoids that increases blood flow in the brain, which helps with mentally challenging tasks. An experiment asked 30 participants to count backward by threes. The subjects were able to do the countdown quicker and more accurately after just having a cup of hot chocolate.

Source: *The Telegraph*

Pepsi was at one point the owner of **17** Russian military submarines

In the 1950s, Pepsi and the Soviet Union arranged a deal to sell the drink in the country. The cola was paid for with vodka. Later, in the 1980s, vodka wasn't worth enough to cover the cost. The Soviet Union traded the drink for military ships, making Pepsi one of the biggest naval powers in the world for a short while, before they sold the fleet to a Swedish company for scrap recycling.

Source: *Business Insider*

Astronauts can vote from space

Astronauts aboard the International Space Station are still able to vote. They get their ballot as an encrypted PDF in their inbox and cast their vote from an onboard computer. It required some tweaking in the laws back on Earth to accommodate for this, but now people in space can vote almost like anyone else.

Source: *The Atlantic*

Prehistoric Britons used human skulls as cups

Three human skulls carefully cut in the shape of drinking cups have been found in a cave in southwest England. It is believed that the Cro-Magnons who were living there thousands of years ago used the cups as part of some sort of ritual.

Source: *BBC News*

About **50 percent** of people admit writing down tasks they have already done on their to-do list just so they can cross them off

While writing a book about to-do lists, author Sasha Cagen conducted a survey on the topic that collected answers from hundreds of participants. After they wrote the completed task down, 66 percent would cross the task off, 21 percent would check it off instead, and 5 percent traced an "X" next to it.

Source: *To-Do List*

Parts of Canada have lower gravity than other parts of the world

The Hudson Bay region and its surrounding areas are missing gravity. Two complementary theories address the mystery. A thick ice sheet used to lie there tens of thousands of years ago, leaving an empty indent on the planet, decreasing its mass in that area. In addition, a layer of magma is dragging down the continental plates in this zone, decreasing its mass further.

Source: *HowStuffWorks*

There was no clear word for the color orange until the 16th century

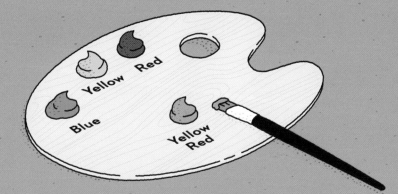

Although the human eye can see millions of colors, human languages only name a few thousand. Orange is one color that got its current name quite late in English, as well as in many other languages. Named after the fruit, the color was formerly referred to with short-lived analogies or thought of as a yellowish-red or reddish-yellow.

Source: *Literary Hub*

The sight of meat calms men down

In a curious experiment, men were placed in front of random pictures while someone read out loud to them. The people reading made mistakes occasionally, and researchers observed the men's responses to those mistakes. The researchers found that the subjects were more tolerant with the readers' errors when they were looking at pictures of meat. Funnily enough, they expected the opposite.

Source: *LA Weekly*

An octopus actually has
6 arms and **2** legs, not **8** legs

An octopus does not have 8 legs, 8 arms, or 8 tentacles, for that matter. It has 2 legs, used for moving around, and 6 arms, used principally for feeding.

Source: *The Telegraph*

The average person will spend **half a year** of their life looking for misplaced items

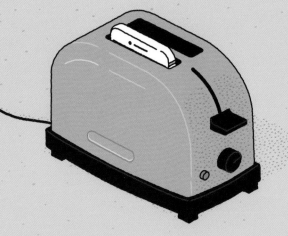

A survey about lost (and found) items estimated that Americans spend about 2.5 days a year looking for things that they have lost. It takes on average 5 minutes to find what they are looking for, and 69 percent end up finding something else that they lost instead.

Source: *Pixie*

Over 400 million years ago, Earth was covered with giant mushrooms that were **24 feet** tall

Long before dinosaurs, in the Silurian and Devonian periods, when the first animals to live outside water were still very new at it, a genus of fungi named *Prototaxites* were growing on Earth. Reaching 24 feet high, they were organized in very thin tubes laced together in trunks that could measure about 3 feet wide.

Source: *Smithsonian Magazine*

Machine-spun cotton candy was invented by a dentist

Making cotton candy was all manual work before 1904. That year, William Morrison, a dentist and capable tinkerer in his spare time, partnered with confectioner John C. Wharton at the World's Fair in St. Louis. They sold "Fairy Floss," the first-ever machine-spun cotton candy, which was very successful.

Source: *Journal of the History of Dentistry*

From 1913 to 1915, parents in the US could mail their kids through the postal service

In 1913, the US Postal Service introduced a new parcel service for items more than 4 pounds, with very loose guidelines on what could or couldn't be sent. As it was often cheaper to buy stamps for their kids than to buy them train tickets, a few parents sent children to relatives through the postal system.

Source: History

The sound of a black hole is a **B-flat** note

(57 octaves lower than the middle C)

Astronomers have been measuring the sound waves emanating from a black hole located in the Perseus galaxy cluster. The black hole continuously hums a single note: a very low B-flat. But its frequency is far too deep to be heard by human ears.

Source: NASA

Left-handed people tend to live shorter lives because almost everything is designed for right-handed people

A study focusing on 1,000 Californians found that the left-handed portion died on average 9 years younger than their right-handed counterparts. They also discovered that left-handers are 5 times more likely to die in an accident than right-handers.

Source: *The New York Times*

There is a giant statue of Jesus in Poland that serves as a Wi-Fi antenna

Christ the King is a statue in western Poland. It stands a few feet taller than the similar but much more famous Cristo Redentor in Rio de Janeiro. It is more tech savvy than its Brazilian counterpart, however; its crown hosts a variety of antennas that broadcast an Internet signal. No one seems to know exactly who or what is using the signals, though.

Source: *Gizmodo*

Many lipsticks contain fish scales

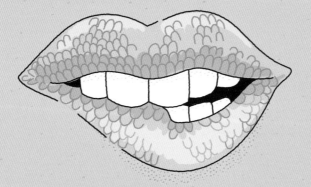

Lipstick can contain a lot of ingredients, for instance, beeswax; carnauba wax from palm trees; lanolin from wool; castor oil from beans; dyes from vegetable, animal, or synthetic origins; and sometimes guanine, a substance that can be found in fish scales. It's what gives the cosmetics a pearl-like appearance.

Source: *BBC Science Focus*

Cheese triggers the same part of the brain as addictive drugs

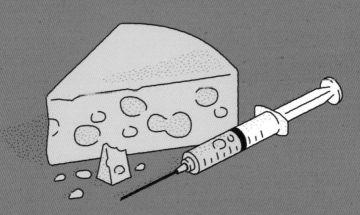

A study found that cheese and dishes containing cheese ranked high in an experiment on addictive food. A reason is that one of the major components of cheese is casein, which produces casomorphins when digested. Casomorphins impact our opioid receptors, the same part of the brain that gets activated when consuming opium or morphine.

Source: *Tech Times*

Whales can get a tan too

Whales can spend hours at the surface of the ocean when they are not diving, and their skin needs protection against the sun. Different species have different strategies. Some types have high levels of melanin to protect their skin. Like humans' skin, however, blue whales can tan during the summer. With the diminishing of the ozone layer, skin diseases among whales and other marine mammals are increasing.

Source: *National Geographic*

A building in Japan has a highway passing through its 5th, 6th, and 7th floors

Osaka is home to the Gate Tower Building, a 16-story tower that opened in 1992. Three of its floors are crossed by a motorway going through a large hole in the building. The road does not touch the building and is held up by a bridge. The building's elevator simply skips from floor 4 to 8.

Source: *Forbes*

The very first game of basketball was played with a soccer ball

In 1891, teacher James Naismith designed a game that would keep his students fit indoors during winter months. He grabbed some empty peach baskets, mounted them on the wall, divided his class of 18 in 2 teams, and established the rules: Throw the soccer ball in the baskets to score, don't run with it, and bring the ladder to get the ball out after each score.

Source: *The Canadian Encyclopedia*

Colgate used to sell candles

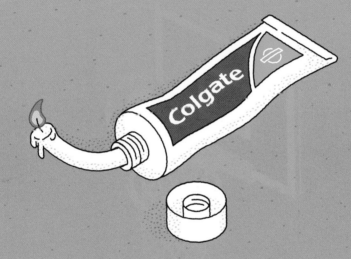

When English immigrant William Colgate founded his company in 1806 in New York City, he was making soap and candles. It was only in 1873, well after his death, that the company started to sell toothpaste, which was originally sold in jars.

Source: Colgate–Palmolive

In the 18th century, you could pay for your ticket to the London Zoo by bringing a cat or a dog to feed to the lions

Beginning in the 1200s, the Tower of London began to host a menagerie of exotic animals. Those animals eventually relocated and became the London Zoo in the 1830s. Before that, the entrance was halfpence, but if you brought a spare cat or dog, you got in for free.

Source: *Londonist*

Russia and America are less than **3 miles** apart at the nearest point

2.4 mi

The Bering Strait in the Pacific Ocean separates Alaska and the easternmost region of Russia. The strait itself is 51 miles wide, but 2 islands there lie only 2.4 miles apart: Little Diomede and Big Diomede, as they are called, belong to the United States and to Russia, respectively.

Source: *Amusing Planet*

Your smartphone is more powerful than the original space shuttle's computers

The onboard computers operating the space shuttle had limited resources, running about 400 KB to 1 MB of memory. A few decades later, current smartphones have a memory between 4 GB and 10 GB, 10,000 times more than the original space shuttle. It shows how much technology has developed and become accessible to most.

Source: *Do Space*

One soccer field of forest was lost every second in 2017

In 2017, the Global Forest Watch reported the loss of 72.6 acres of forest in a year—an area equivalent to the size of Italy—due to humans cutting down trees and natural disasters like forest fires. Per second, the surface being destroyed was more than a soccer field. That amount of tree destruction is a massive threat both to climate and to wildlife.

Source: *The Guardian*

Some dinosaur noises in *Jurassic Park* were made from recordings of mating tortoises

Gary Rydstrom, sound designer for *Jurassic Park*, went to Marine World to record tortoises mating. He used these noises for the velociraptors' groaning sounds. But they were not the only animals dubbing the dinosaurs: A whole menagerie of dogs, horses, donkeys, geese, swans, owls, cows, dolphins, baby elephants, and humans gave their voices to the creatures.

Source: *Vulture*

Kellogg's All-Bran is only **87 percent bran**

The back of an All-Bran breakfast cereal box reads as follows: "Ingredients: Wheat Bran (87 percent), Sugar, Barley Malt Flavoring, Salt, Vitamins & Minerals: Niacin, Iron, Vitamin B_6, Vitamin B_2 (Riboflavin), Vitamin B_1 (Thiamin), Folic Acid, Vitamin D, Vitamin B_{12}."

Source: *Open Food Facts*

On a timeline, the *T. rex* is closer to humans than it is to the *Stegosaurus*

We often think of dinosaurs as living all together some time far in the past. But an early dinosaur like *Stegosaurus* actually lived about 150 million years ago, while a later specimen like *Tyrannosaurus* lived around 67 million years ago. The earliest humans appeared 4 million years ago.

Source: *Smithsonian Magazine*

Cleaning the house with toxic cleaners is as harmful for the health as smoking 1 pack of cigarettes

Cleaning exposes your lungs to chemical sprays and other potentially toxic agents, which cause damage to respiratory health in the long term. People working as cleaners, who are exposed constantly, are especially vulnerable. A study found that over time, the impairment caused by cleaning is similar to that caused by smoking cigarettes.

Source: American Thoracic Society

The word people in the United States most often Google how to spell is "beautiful"

Q hwo 2 spel butifl

Google released a list of the words people in the United States most often look up how to spell. The most searched spelling is "beautiful" (in California, Kentucky, Minnesota, New York, and Ohio), followed by "pneumonia" (in Alabama, Maine, Michigan, and Washington). Mary Poppins's made-up "supercalifragilisticexpialidocious" topped the list in Connecticut and West Virginia. And the most searched word in Wisconsin is "Wisconsin."

Source: *The Washington Post*

Before 1977, tourists were allowed to climb the stones at Stonehenge

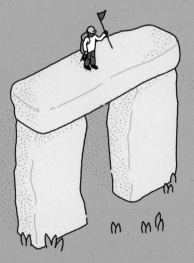

The prehistoric monument of Stonehenge in England was built thousands of years ago and is believed to be a sacred burial ground. The site has always attracted visitors, but was protected only recently. Before that, people would chisel off bits of rocks to take home as souvenirs, and they were indeed allowed to climb on the stones.

Source: *Smithsonian Magazine*

The start-up music for Windows 95 was composed on a Mac

(by Brian Eno)

Previous versions of Windows software had a short bugle-like "Tada!" sound when your computer was ready to use. For Windows 95, Microsoft went for something more welcoming and elaborate. They hired Brian Eno, a famed English musician, to compose the tune. He worked on 84 iterations, opting for harps and bells with strings in the background, all on his Macintosh.

Source: *Neowin*

Some species of starfish can regenerate a whole body from a single arm

Most starfish can regenerate bits of their body if damaged, and some can regenerate a full limb if lost. A few, however, can even regrow fully from a single remaining limb. The process can take months to years, and the animal is very vulnerable during that time.

Source: *UCSB ScienceLine*

A group of ferrets is called a business

The English language is very creative when it comes to naming groups of animals: a flock of birds, a herd of cows, and so on. Some names get more interesting and amusing: a murder of crows, a wisdom of wombats, a mischief of rats, a parliament of owls, a conspiracy of meerkats, an implausibility of gnus, and, indeed, a business of ferrets.

Source: *Zoological World*

The world's longest pedal-powered tandem bicycle has **52** seats

It started with 2 sisters liking the same boy, arguing about which of them would ride their tandem bicycle with him. To solve the matter, their father welded an extra frame and seat onto a bicycle. They later got carried away and added seats after seats, until the bike reached a length of 138 feet.

Source: *Active*

Everyone has a unique tongue print, just as they do fingerprints

Research on "tongue biometrics" has been conducted, and, while not widely in use yet, prototypes have been developed for systems verifying people's identities using the physiology of their tongue. At some point in the future, you might be able to unlock your phone by licking it.

Source: Springer Nature

The longest nipple hair ever recorded was **6.7 inches** and belonged to a man in Italy

Daniele Tuveri, an Italian man living in Cagliari, was proudly awarded the world record for the longest nipple hair in 2013. One hair on his right nipple was measured to be 6.7 inches.

Source: *Guinness World Records*

The world's shortest escalator is located in Kawasaki, Japan

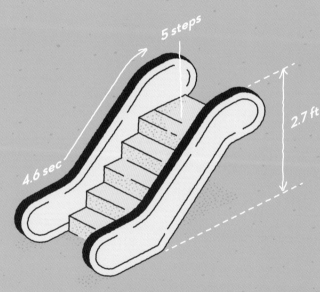

5 steps

4.6 sec

2.7 ft

The city of Kawasaki, midway between Tokyo and Yokohama, hosts a department store named More's, which houses the world's shortest escalator, a 2.7-foot-high, 4.6-second-long ride located in the basement. It's an alternative to the 5-step staircase placed next to it.

Source: *Japan Travel*

Flamingos can drink near-boiling water

Many flamingos live in lakes with high concentrations of salt, which is unsafe for them to drink. For some, their only source of fresh water is geysers, which are hot water and steam that spray out from the earth. Flamingos therefore adapted to be able to drink this water source, which has a temperature approaching boiling point (212°F).

Source: SeaWorld

We hold 0.001 carats of gold inside us

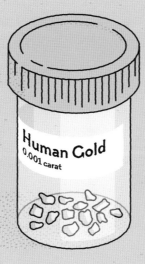

A person weighing 150 pounds contains about 94 pounds of oxygen, 35 pounds of carbon, 7 pounds of hydrogen...and 0.001 carats (about 7 millionths of an ounce) of gold.

Source: Gold Traders

Happy pizza is a pizza sold in Cambodia topped with marijuana

Even though it has been prohibited as a drug since the 1990s, cannabis is still legally in use in Cambodia as a medicinal plant and as an aromatic herb. And it's this latter use that interests us here: In the capital city of Phnom Penh, many pizza places offer an unusual specialty: cannabis pizza.

Source: *Culture Trip*

Nike's swoosh logo was purchased in 1971 for **$35**

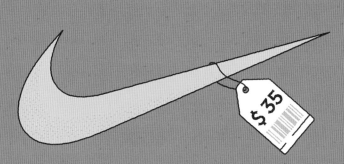

In the late 1960s, Carolyn Davidson, then a design student in Portland, got a gig from a new sportswear company, one that would eventually be known as Nike. Asked to create their new logo, she designed a few samples, including the one that is now one of the world's most recognized symbols, and got paid this small sum.

Source: CNBC

Wine glasses are **7 times** larger than they used to be

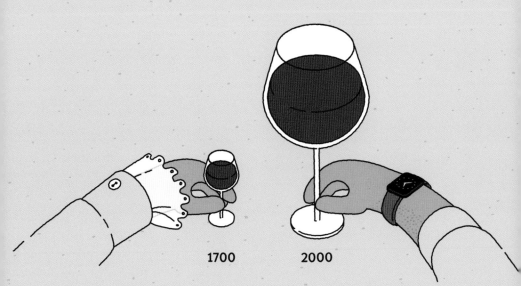

1700   2000

The average wine glass from the 1700s was about 2.2 fluid ounces, but that jumped to 14 fluid ounces in the 2000s. Researchers compared 411 glasses from the past 300 years, found in museums, catalogs, and other sources, and concluded that glasses got 6–7 times larger during that time, especially in the last few decades.

Source: *The Guardian*

The oldest known customer complaint was written on a clay tablet in Mesopotamia **4,000** years ago

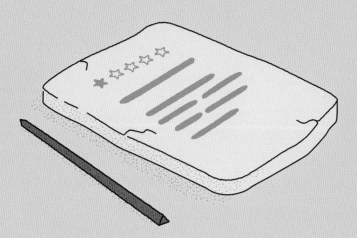

Nanni was a copper merchant whose complaint about a bad deal was not only ignored; the money was also never refunded, even after Nanni sent several messengers (through a war zone!). "How can you treat somebody like me with such contempt?" Nanni traced angrily on a clay tablet in 1750 B.C.

Source: *Ancient Origins*

From 1945 to 1947, a rooster named Mike lived **18 months** without a head

When Colorado farmers chopped the head off this chicken, he stayed alive. The cut spared parts of his brain. They decided to keep him and called him Mike. The fowl made a sensation and became a local celebrity. The farmers even made some money showing Mike around the country, until one day he choked and died.

Source: *BBC News*

Each day **$6 million** is shredded and turned into compost

Paper money that is torn or damaged gets removed from circulation and shredded. In the United States, $6 million in paper money is cut into small pieces daily. Piles of money scraps used to end up in landfills but are now brought to a compost facility where they are blended with other waste before being turned into soil.

Source: *CNET*

Trees can send secret warning signals to other trees about incoming insect attacks

Plants can indeed communicate with one another. Some correspond by emitting volatile organic chemicals, while some prefer sending electric signals. Their messages can have different meanings, such as alerting about insects, advising good directions in which to grow, or regulating the collective temperature.

Source: *Quanta Magazine*

Global wind speeds have been declining since 1960

Back then

Today

Winds on Earth are slowing down, and scientists are trying to figure out why. Looking at data starting in 1960, they found that the average wind speed has decreased by 0.3 miles per hour every decade. The phenomenon might become a problem for several reasons, including issues generating power and dispersing pollution out of cities.

Source: *Horizon*

Pineapples once were status symbols in Western countries

(they were so expensive that people rented them for the evening to show off at parties)

Christopher Columbus brought the pineapple to Europe from his travels to South America in the 15th century, but it didn't acclimate well to the local conditions. By the 17th century, pineapples were still rare there and considered very luxurious, with 1 fruit costing up to $8,000 in today's money.

Source: *Mental Floss*

We touch our faces
15.7 times an hour on average

A study performed in 2008 in California on 10 subjects performing everyday office tasks showed that they were on average touching their faces 15.7 times an hour. If we consider a sleeping time of 8 hours, that means the average person touches their face about 250 times a day during waking hours.

Source: *Journal of Occupational and Environmental Hygiene*

We fart about **18** fluid ounces of gas every day

A study conducted in 1941, "The Quantity of Colonic Flatus Excreted by the 'Normal' Individual," involved the insertion of rubber tubes with balloons into 5 men who volunteered. The study concluded that the subjects farted an average volume of 17.8 fluid ounces of gas daily.

Source: *The American Journal of Digestive Diseases*

Women are more productive
at warmer temperatures

(the opposite is true for men)

HR Department

In a study, 543 subjects performed tasks at various temperatures. The conclusion: Women are on average less productive at colder temperatures (under 70°F) and more productive at warmer temperatures (over 80°F). Men are the opposite, but they lose less productivity in the warm temperatures than women do in the cold. Both work the same in temperatures in between.

Source: University of Southern California

Some ant species developed agriculture millions of years before humans and live on mushrooms that they cultivate themselves

Several species of ants, named attines, started farming 55–60 million years before humans did. Their favorite food? Fungus. They organized themselves around cutting wild leaves, bringing them back to their colony, looking after the fungus that grows on it, and finally harvesting and eating the fungus. Interestingly, fungus species have evolved in sync with ant species.

Source: National Academy of Sciences

There is a basketball court above the courtroom of the Supreme Court

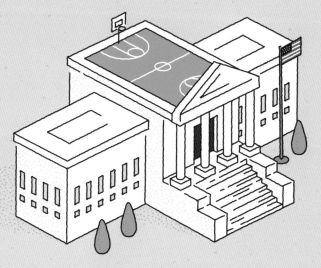

The US Supreme Court building, built in 1935 in Washington, DC, does not only house a courtroom. Its fifth floor also houses a gym, equipped with a basketball court, amusingly referred to as "the highest court in the land."

Source: *Axios*

Phones are dirtier than toilet seats

Most people don't clean their phone, yet they touch it about 3,000 times a day. That's a lot less cleaning and a lot more touching than for a toilet seat or a flush. A study indeed found a higher level of bacteria, yeast, and mold on phones than on toilets.

Source: Insurance2go

France didn't stop executing people by guillotine until **1977**

(the year of *Saturday Night Fever*)

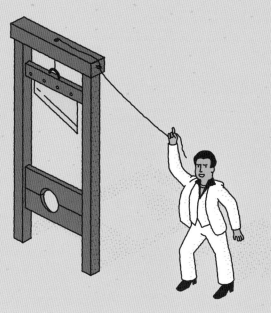

On September 10, 1977, torturer and murderer Hamida Djandoubi was executed by guillotine. It was the last time the instrument was used in France since its introduction in the 18th century, and the death penalty was abolished soon after. A few months later, on December 14, 1977, *Saturday Night Fever* with John Travolta started playing in cinemas.

Source: *Wired*

Hamsters on a wheel can run more than **5 miles** a night

Hamsters and other rodents are cursorial animals: They need to run a lot. That's why wheels are often mounted in rodents' cages. Studies have recorded the lengths traveled by hamsters in their wheels, and 5.6 miles is not an unusual distance for one of their nightly runs.

Source: *Animal Behaviour*

Scientists can turn peanut butter into diamonds

(because of its high carbon content)

In studying how Earth was formed in its early days, scientists investigated how diamonds were formed from sources of carbon under high pressure. Using powerful presses, they crushed and cooked minerals and gases until they turned into diamonds. And they did it once with peanut butter, which contains a lot of carbon.

Source: *BBC Future*

Australian drivers in Queensland can get an emoji on their car's license plate

As of 2019, drivers can pay a fee and choose from five emoji to add to their license plate: the smiley face, the winking face, the "laughing out loud" face, the "cool sunglasses" face, and the "heart eyes" face. License plates will still need to feature some numbers and letters as well.

Source: *Business Insider*

The toothbrush was invented in 1498 in China

1438

1450

1498

1500

1524

Cleaning your teeth in ancient times wasn't so easy: You could wipe them with a cloth, chew on a piece of twig, or carve your own toothpicks. In 1498, however, the emperor of China patented a toothbrush made of hog hair with a handle in bone or bamboo. The new method took off slowly, but it eventually became the worldwide standard.

Source: *Wired*

Sea otters have pockets in their skin where they keep food and rocks for crushing seashells

Sea otters eat sea urchins, mollusks, crustaceans, fish, shellfish, clams, and so on. But they often have to break outer shells to get to the meat under them. They have a pouch of skin under each foreleg where they can store food, along with a rock or two to break open harder shells.

Source: *Ocean Today*

The inventor of Vaseline ate a spoonful of it every day

Chemist Robert Chesebrough discovered petroleum jelly and its healing properties in the 1850s, then trademarked it under the name Vaseline. To promote the product, he would drive around New York, burn himself in public, then apply Vaseline on the wound to show its efficacy. He also ate a spoonful of it a day.

Source: *Age of Awareness*

There are no stop signs in Paris

Even though it boasts more than 2 million inhabitants and a considerable number of cars, the French metropolis has managed to do just fine without any stop signs. The last known stop sign disappeared in the 2010s. At any unmarked crossing, cars coming from the right have the right-of-way, and bigger intersections have traffic lights.

Source: *Reader's Digest*

A Japanese toilet brand has built a motorcycle that runs on excrement

The toilet manufacturer Toto created a prototype of a 3-wheeled motorcycle, the Toilet Bike Neo. Its source of fuel? Bio-gas created by purifying methane, itself extracted from livestock "waste," i.e., poop. Three years of research was needed to develop the vehicle.

Source: *Wired*

The current US flag was designed by a high school student for a class project

(he got a B, which was changed to an A after the US Congress accepted the design as the national flag)

The US flag has had more or less the same design since the 18th century. Each time the number of states changed, the number of stars and their layout changed too. When the addition of Alaska and Hawaii necessitated a 50-star design, student Robert Heft spent a weekend cutting and sewing a design, which was adopted as the official flag in 1960.

Source: Chamber of Commerce

There are hundreds of dead bodies on Mount Everest

More than 300 people have died on Everest since it was first climbed about a century ago. Since removing the bodies is a dangerous enterprise in itself, most are kept on the mountain, frozen on location. Recently, climbing the summit has become more popular, leading the paths to be overcrowded and the risk to be higher.

Source: *Business Insider*

"Hello" didn't become a greeting until the telephone arrived

Hello?

"Ahoy" would be the first thing you say on the phone if Alexander Graham Bell's preferences were still followed. Rather, it is "Hello," which was previously used to express surprise or call for attention. Thomas Edison preferred "Hello," and the greeting was printed in early telephone guides. It then spread beyond the telephone lines to become the universal greeting we know now.

Source: NPR

Female kangaroos have **3 vaginas**

All marsupials, including kangaroos and koalas, share the same female reproductive system: They have 3 vaginas: 2 side ones for reproduction, each leading to a separate uterus, and a middle one for giving birth.

Source: *Discover*

IKEA sells a BILLY bookcase every **5** seconds

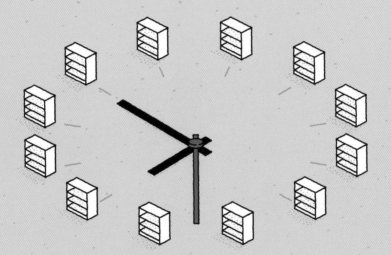

IKEA estimates that they sell a copy of their most popular bookshelves collection, launched in 1979, every 5 seconds. The factory that produces it, Gyllensvaans Möbler in southern Sweden, produces about 1 bookcase every 3 seconds.

Source: IKEA

There is a city called "Batman" in Turkey

Batman, capital of the Batman province and home of the Batman University and the Batman football club, is a city in southeastern Turkey, named after the river flowing nearby. Worth noting is that a few hundred miles away from the city, one can find another village of Batman, but this one is in Iran.

Source: *Encyclopedia Britannica*

To find out how dinosaurs walked, scientists have been sticking fake tails on chickens

It's no secret that today's birds are descendants of what used to be dinosaurs. To study the locomotion of dinosaurs, researchers realized that by moving the center of gravity of chickens backward with artificial tails, beginning from their hatching to their adulthood, they could get the fowl to walk more or less like dinosaurs used to.

Source: *PLOS One*

Our eyes are closed for roughly **10 percent** of our waking hours

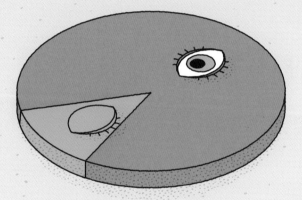

We blink 15–20 times a minute, more than what we need to keep our eyes moist. Researchers discovered another reason for blinking: The brain switches to some sort of idle state during the blink. It does not have to focus and process any visual information for a fraction of a second, thus giving the mind some rest.

Source: *Huffington Post*

You'd have to click the mouse
10 million times to burn 1 calorie

A physics teacher did the calculation: Assuming that it takes a force of 0.1 pounds to click a mouse and that the distance moved by the button being pressed is 0.05 inches, the energy you'll spend is about 0.1 millionth of a calorie. You would need to click 10 million times to burn 1 calorie.

Source: *Wired*

The first shopping cart was made from a folding chair with a basket on the seat and wheels on the legs

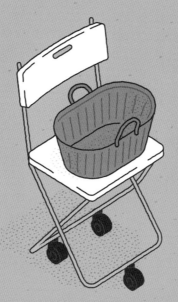

In 1937, the owner of a self-service store, a relatively new concept at that time, was sitting on his chair thinking about how customers could carry more groceries at a time. He had a eureka moment: He put a basket on the chair, called a mechanic for help, and built the first prototype, which proved very successful.

Source: *Wired*

If the sun were the size of a tennis ball, Earth would be the size of a grain of sand

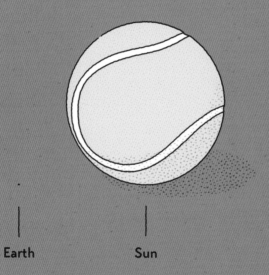

Earth   Sun

Earth is 7,926 miles wide, and the sun is 864,900 miles wide. If we imagine scaling the sun down to 3 inches, Earth would be more than 100 times smaller, or 0.03 inches in diameter.

Source: Johns Hopkins University

The Beatles use the word "love"
613 times in their songs

All you need is love

And I love her

Can't buy me love

Hallelujah, I love her so

I'm in love

It's only love

Love me do

Love of the loved

Love you to

PS I love you

Real love

She loves you

So how come (No one loves me)

Soldier of love

Step inside love

Sure to fall (

To k

If you count the words appearing through the 300 or so songs by the Beatles, you'll find the most used word is "you" with 2,262 occurrences, followed by "I," "the," "to," "me," "and," and "a," and all are pronouns, prepositions, and the like. Finally, a much more interesting word arrives at the 8th place: "love," with 613 appearances.

Source: *The Guardian*

One hamburger may contain meat from **100** different cows

Cow #15

Cow #34

Cow #71

Cow #83

Cow #100

In the highly industrial process of producing meat, hamburger patties are not made from the meat of a single cattle. After the slaughter, the meat is mixed and mashed together when minced into ground beef. McDonald's notably confirmed that its beef was made from the meat of more than a hundred different cows.

Source: *The Washington Post*

Steve Jobs chose the name Apple because it would be placed before Atari in the phone book

When Steve Jobs and Steve Wozniak created Apple in 1976, the former came up with the name Apple for 2 reasons: He'd had a nice experience working in an apple orchard a few years earlier, and the name would put them before Atari in the phone book, the company where Jobs worked previously.

Source: *The Atlantic*

Airplanes fly slower today than they did in the past

1973

2019

A flight from New York to Houston in 1973 took about 2.5 hours. It now takes almost 4 hours. One reason has to do with fuel consumption: Flying slower uses less fuel, and airlines can save money this way. Another reason is that airlines preventively plan for generous flight times to avoid being late.

Source: *The Telegraph*

Money shaped like knives was used in China 2,500 years ago

Around 600 to 200 B.C., various kingdoms in China used dull knives as a currency. The origin of this practice supposedly has to do with people running low on money, so they traded knives. Years later, actual "knife money" was being cast from bronze. Meanwhile, in another part of China, people were using spade-shaped money.

Source: *Calgary Coin Gallery*

Neil Armstrong's boots are still in space

On July 20, 1969, the lunar module landed, with Buzz Aldrin and Neil Armstrong on board. They walked, said some inspiring words, and planted a flag. Then they had to go home, but first they had to lose some weight from the spacecraft, especially since they had picked up some moon rocks to take back to Earth. Neil Armstrong's boots were jettisoned to lighten the load.

Source: NASA

There is a town in Michigan called "Hell"

Officially adopting the name in 1841, this diabolically named hamlet offers a couple of theories about how it came to be called this in the first place. In one, German visitors described the town as *"So schön hell!"* ("So beautifully bright!") In another one, early settlers simply found the natural conditions there absolutely infernal.
Source: *H2G2*

In 1930s London, babies were dangled out of windows in cages

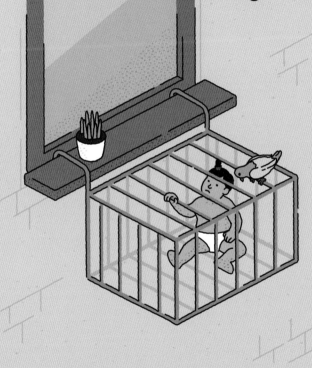

Fresh air: That is the reason London parents living in flats a hundred years ago would purchase cages similar to chicken coops, literally named "baby cages," put their little kids in them, and hang them out the window.

Source: *Good Housekeeping*

A can of Diet Coke will float in water, while a can of regular Coke will sink

Due to different concentrations in sugar (about 1.4 ounces per can for regular Coke and almost none for Diet Coke), both drinks have different densities. Regular Coke is denser than water, resulting in a can sinking, while Diet Coke is less dense, allowing it to float at the surface.

Source: *Mental Floss*

Cheerleading started as an all-male activity

Cheerleading can be traced back to the late 18th century, when male students started practicing sports in universities. It's only in 1923 that the University of Minnesota allowed women to join the activity, most others following much later in the 1940s. By the 1970s, most cheerleaders were women.

Source: *International Cheer Union*

The inventor of the web rotary press was killed by his own invention

Printing has a rich and black-and-white history, including this bit from the 1860s: William Bullock, an inventor known for improving the rotary press and turning it into a machine capable of printing up to 12,000 pages an hour, died after he kicked his invention and got his leg caught and crushed in the device.

Source: *Prepressure*

One of Samsung's first products was dried fish

From 1938, when it was founded in Daegu, South Korea, until 1969, when it started making TV sets, the Samsung company did not produce electronics. Instead, it started as a food exporter, shipping products such as dried fish and flour to China, before expanding into other industries like life insurance, textiles, and, finally, electronics.

Source: *Business Insider*

Boanthropy is the psychological disorder of someone who believes they are a cow

Someone who suffers from boanthropy lives in a delusional state, believing themselves to be a cow or another bovine, and attempting to behave like one.

Source: *The Pharmaceutical Journal*

A lemon will float in water, but a lime will sink

The density of a lemon is less than that of a lime: Compared to water, a lime is denser. That's the reason limes and lemons react differently when placed in water.

Source: Indian Ministry of Human Resource Development

Gold is edible

Pure gold can be eaten. Since it is chemically inert, it is not absorbed by the body. It is actually an approved food additive in the form of thin leaves. It has been added to drinks since the Renaissance, is found in some candies and pastries, and has been wrapping the patty of a $666 hamburger in New York.

Source: *Slate*

China owns nearly all of the pandas in the world and rents them out for about **$1 million** a year

Most giant pandas on Earth belong to China. The ones in captivity across the world are actually rented out to zoos by the Chinese government, often with a 10-year agreement. On top of paying to rent the pandas, zoos have to grow a lot of bamboo, which constitutes 99 percent of a panda's diet.

Source: *Business Insider*

Eggplants contain nicotine

Doctors have measured the amount of nicotine in plants of the nightshade family, which includes tobacco, eggplants, tomatoes, and potatoes. All these plants contain nicotine; for instance, 22 pounds of eggplants have as much nicotine as 1 cigarette.

Source: *Huffington Post*

There are **300,000** items in the average American home

4,501

#234,502

#234,503

#234,504

#234,505

#234,506

#23

Professional organizer Regina Lark estimated this total number of objects in the average US household. Another statistic is about US kids: They represent 3.7 percent of the international children population, but own 47 percent of all the toys and kids' books.
Source: *Los Angeles Times*

Craving more facts?

Check out our website **Factourism.com** or follow us
at **@factourism** on *Instagram*, *Twitter*, and *Facebook*.
We publish new facts frequently!

Sources

Each one of our facts comes from an article we have read. Want to know about some of them in further detail? Type in these short links, and you will be automatically redirected to our original source.

p 124 factourism.com/source/otters-pockets-b
p 125 factourism.com/source/vaseline-spoon-b
p 126 factourism.com/source/paris-stop
p 127 factourism.com/source/toilet-motorcycle
p 128 factourism.com/source/us-flag
p 129 factourism.com/source/dead-climbers
p 130 factourism.com/source/hello
p 131 factourism.com/source/kangaroo-vaginas
p 132 factourism.com/source/billy-seconds
p 133 factourism.com/source/batman-city-b
p 134 factourism.com/source/chicken-dinosaur
p 135 factourism.com/source/closed-eyes
p 136 factourism.com/source/mouse-fitness
p 137 factourism.com/source/shopping-chair-b
p 138 factourism.com/source/tennis-sun
p 139 factourism.com/source/beatles-love
p 140 factourism.com/source/hamburger-cows
p 141 factourism.com/source/apple-phonebook
p 142 factourism.com/source/flying-speed
p 143 factourism.com/source/knife-money-b
p 144 factourism.com/source/space-boots
p 145 factourism.com/source/hell-town-b
p 146 factourism.com/source/baby-cage
p 147 factourism.com/source/diet-coke-floating
p 148 factourism.com/source/male-cheerleader-b
p 149 factourism.com/source/mortuary-press
p 150 factourism.com/source/samsung-fish
p 151 factourism.com/source/cow-disorder-b
p 152 factourism.com/source/lemon-lime
p 153 factourism.com/source/edible-gold
p 154 factourism.com/source/renting-pandas
p 155 factourism.com/source/eggplant-nicotine
p 156 factourism.com/source/american-home